DATE DUE

DEMCO 38-297

ARTISTS AND WRITERS OF THE HARLEM RENAISSANCE

The *Collective Biographies* Series

Collective Biographies

ARTISTS AND WRITERS OF THE HARLEM RENAISSANCE

Wendy Hart Beckman

Enslow Publishers, Inc.

40 Industrial Road   PO Box 38
Box 398   Aldershot
Berkeley Heights, NJ 07922   Hants GU12 6BP
USA   UK

http://www.enslow.com

To Homer L. Meade, my wonderful high school English teacher. You introduced me to Langston Hughes and the Harlem Renaissance. I remember—you smiled. My life will never be the same.

—whb

Library of Congress Cataloging-in-Publication Data

Beckman, Wendy Hart.
    Artists and writers of the Harlem Renaissance / by Wendy Hart Beckman.
        p. cm. — (Collective biographies)
    Contents: James Weldon Johnson—Alain LeRoy Locke—Zora Neale Hurston—Bessie Smith—Aaron Douglas—Duke Ellington—Arna Bontemps—Countee Cullen—Josphine Baker.
    Includes bibliographical references and index.
    ISBN 0-7660-1834-2
    1. Harlem Renaissance. 2. African Americans—Biography.
[1. Harlem Renaissance. 2. Artists. 3. Authors, American. 4. African Americans—Biography.] I. Title. II. Series.
NX512.3.A35 B43 2001
700'.92'39607307471—dc21
                                                        2001001309

This book profiles the lives of ten Artists and Writers of the Harlem Renaissance, including James Weldon Johnson, Alain LeRoy Locke, Zora Neale Hurston, Bessie Smith, Aaron Douglas, Duke Ellington, Langston Hughes, Arna Bontemps, Countee Cullen and Josephine Baker.

Printed in the United States of America

10 9 8 7 6 5 4 3 2

To Our Readers:
We have done our best to make sure all Internet addresses in this book were active and appropriate when we went to press. However, the author and the publisher have no control over and assume no liability for the material available on those Internet sites or on other Web sites they may link to. Any comments or suggestions can be sent by e-mail to comments@enslow.com or to the address on the back cover.

Contents

THE CRISIS

A RECORD OF THE DARKER RACES

Volume One   MARCH, 1911   Number Five

Edited by W. E. BURGHARDT DU BOIS, with the co-operation of Oswald Garrison Villard, J. Max Barber, Charles Edward Russell, Kelly Miller, W. S. Braithwaite and M. D. Maclean.

Egyptian Portrait of One of the Black Kings of the Upper Nile, Ra-Maat-Neb, Builder of Pyramid No. 17. (After Lepsius.)

PUBLISHED MONTHLY BY THE

National Association for the Advancement of Colored People

AT TWENTY VESEY STREET   NEW YORK CITY

ONE DOLLAR A YEAR   TEN CENTS A COPY

The Crisis magazine was a tool for African-American writers, poets, and artists to share their work. It was read by people all over the world.

Preface

In the early 1900s, there arose a remarkable period of creativity in the black community centered in the Harlem section of New York City. African-American art, literature, music, and social commentary flourished during the 1920s and 1930s. Attracting both black and white sponsors and audiences, this cultural movement became known as the Harlem Renaissance.

"Sterling Brown [a Renaissance writer], has identified five themes animating the movement: (1) Africa as a source of race pride, (2) black American heroes, (3) racial political propaganda, (4) the black folk tradition, and (5) candid self-revelation."[1]

At the core of the Harlem Renaissance was a group of older African Americans from the National Association for the Advancement of Colored People (NAACP), the National Urban League (NUL), and various universities and journals. Around this group were the writers and artists who represented the young heart and soul of the New Negro movement. In addition, there was another group made up of other writers and artists who participated at various times but were not pivotal to the movement.

W.E.B. Du Bois, the influential editor of the NAACP magazine *The Crisis*, coined the term "Talented Tenth," referring to the elite tenth of a percent of the black community.[2] This group was mostly "Episcopalian or Presbyterian; was Republican; owned their homes; were lawyers, doctors, and dentists; [and] attended Fisk, Howard, or Atlanta [universities]. . . ."[3] The Talented Tenth was one of the major forces of the Harlem Renaissance.

According to historian David Levering Lewis, two things made the Harlem Renaissance possible: demography and repression.[4] A great black migration had begun from the rural South to the industrial North as African Americans sought new jobs and new freedom. Racial tensions rose and major race riots occurred across northern cities in 1919.

The Talented Tenth of Harlem reacted by seeking to create the image of the "New Negro." The founding fathers of the Harlem Renaissance realized that the blacks' access to commerce, politics, and property was blocked. Two paths remained opened to them: arts and letters. There were, however, opposing forces within the Harlem Renaissance with differing philosophies as to the role of black art and literature. Although many of the writers and artists did not share a common purpose, their work all reflected black life from a black point of view.

There were three major phases of the Harlem Renaissance. The first phase, which ended around 1923, was highly influenced by white artists and writers who were interested in black culture.

The second phase, from about 1924 to 1926, began when more blacks began to express their creativity and philosophy themselves. The NUL and the NAACP and their magazines, *Opportunity* and *The Crisis*, dominated this phase. Both these organizations believed that arts and letters were only good as propaganda tools for the advancement of blacks. The second phase also marked collaboration between the Talented Tenth and the white "Negrotarians" (as writer Zora Neale Hurston called them).

The third phase, from mid-1926 to March 1935, was dominated by what Hurston called the "Niggerati"—prolific black writers and artists.[5] This last phase marked a rebellion against the civil rights leaders and pushed art for art's sake.

During the Renaissance, Harlem became the place to see and be seen. Langston Hughes, a leading Renaissance writer, described the atmosphere in his first autobiography, *The Big Sea*:

> It was the period when the Negro was in vogue. . . . But I thought it wouldn't last long. . . . For how could a large and enthusiastic number of people be crazy about Negroes forever? But some Harlemites . . . thought the race problem had at last been solved. . . . They were sure the New Negro would lead a new life from then on in green pastures of tolerance. . . . I don't know what made any Negroes think that—except that they were mostly intellectuals doing the thinking.[6]

To celebrate the voices of this new Harlem creative movement, the NAACP threw a benefit party. There Langston Hughes met the influential Charles S. Johnson, editor of the NUL's new magazine *Opportunity*. "Mr. Johnson, I believe, did more to encourage and develop Negro writers during the 1920s than anyone else in America," said Hughes. "Jessie Fauset at *The Crisis*, Charles Johnson at *Opportunity*, and Alain Locke in Washington were the three people who midwifed the so-called New Negro literature into being."[7]

In 1924, Charles S. Johnson threw a party at New York City's Civic Club. He invited a group of influential white writers, editors, publishers, and businessmen to introduce them to a comparable group of equally talented African Americans. Such a mingling between the races was virtually unheard of at the time. Johnson believed that the white publishing world knew very little about the wealth of talent among blacks. The exchange was phenomenal and electrified the African-American literary community. Suddenly it became fashionable to be an African-American artist.

In 1931, at the funeral of A'Lelia Walker, a famous black party hostess, Langston Hughes noted, "That was really the end of the gay times of the New Negro era in Harlem, the period that had begun to reach its end when the crash [Great Depression] came in 1929 and the white people had much less money to spend on themselves, and practically none to spend on

Negroes, for the depression brought everybody down a peg or two. And the Negroes had but few pegs to fall."[8]

The Harlem riot of March 19, 1935, brought the Renaissance to an end. As a result of tensions leading to boycotts and picketing, violence erupted after a young boy was beaten for shoplifting. Three people were killed that night and $2 million worth of damage was done.

It is difficult to quantify the effect of the Harlem Renaissance, but one can start by looking at what was produced during this period. In the area of literature alone, twenty-six novels were written as well as ten volumes of poetry, five Broadway plays, numerous nonfiction books, essays and short stories, and three performed ballets. This was in addition to the contribution of artistic works in the form of musical compositions, concerts, paintings, sculptures, murals, and photographs—an amazing record of creative accomplishment!

James Weldon Johnson

1

James Weldon Johnson
(1871–1938)

The success of the Harlem Renaissance was due, in part, to the older and established writers like James Weldon Johnson who helped and encouraged younger artists and writers. Johnson influenced many young black writers to come to Harlem to be part of the Renaissance movement. He provided them with contacts with his white editors working in white publications. Although Johnson was already in his fifties when the Harlem Renaissance began to bloom, he bloomed right along with it.[1]

James Weldon Johnson was multitalented: He was a poet, novelist, editor, historian, diplomat, attorney, civil rights leader, and National Association for the Advancement of Colored People (NAACP) official. But he is probably best remembered as the lyricist for the song "Lift Every Voice and Sing."

James Weldon Johnson was born in Jacksonville, Florida, on June 17, 1871, to James and Helen Dillet Johnson. He was the middle of three children. His younger brother, John Rosamond Johnson, became a well-known composer of music and teamed up with James to create over two hundred songs.[2]

James's father, a waiter, had been born free and was of mixed ancestry. James's mother had been born in the West Indies of Haitian and French ancestry. She was the first black female teacher in the state of Florida.[3] She taught at Stanton, a segregated school, which James attended through the eighth grade.

There were no black high schools in Jacksonville, so the Johnsons sent James to Atlanta, Georgia, for high school. After graduating, James attended Atlanta University and received a bachelor's degree in 1894. He wanted any education he received to be used to further the interests of black peoples.[4]

Johnson then returned to Jacksonville to become principal of the Stanton Elementary School. By the age of twenty-four, he had founded and was directing a large, all-black high school.[5] At the same time, he studied law, and in 1897 became the first African American admitted to the bar in Florida.

In addition, during this period Johnson founded *The Daily American* in 1895, the first African-American newspaper in the United States. It lasted only a year, but it gave Johnson a place in which to write about racial issues.[6] In his newspaper, Johnson addressed issues of namelessness, the role of black mothers, racial self-hatred, and the idea of a white benefactor who appears in many novels written by black authors.

Before the Harlem Renaissance, Johnson was one of the most well-known African-American writers. His poetry reflected the common themes that were considered "allowable" or "acceptable" to a white audience: pity and humor. Johnson's early poems were often written in black dialect, which is a stereotype of the speech of southern blacks. Black and white critics alike criticized dialect poetry, but Johnson valued the idea of showing all levels of black culture accurately.[7] Johnson later changed his mind and rejected dialect poetry as an effective way to express the black experience.

In 1899, to celebrate Abraham Lincoln's birthday, Johnson wrote the poem "Lift Every Voice and Sing," which his brother Rosamond then set to music the next year. The song became known as the Negro national anthem in the 1940s.[8]

Johnson and his brother Rosamond moved to New York around 1900 to seek out new markets for their songs. However, influential black spokesmen such as Booker T. Washington, educator and reformer, and W.E.B. Du Bois, sociologist and editor, felt that Johnson could better use his talents by taking an important role in the New Negro movement. Johnson was seen as the man who could unite all the separate factions within the movement.

In 1906, through the influence of Booker T. Washington, Johnson was appointed U.S. consul to Puerto Cabello, Venezuela, and in 1909 as U.S. consul in Corinto, Nicaragua. His diplomatic assignments were considered a reward for writing President Theodore Roosevelt's campaign song, "You're All Right, Teddy."[9] During his time as a U.S. consul, Johnson continued his writing and had several poems published.

Johnson returned to the United States in 1910 and married Grace Nail, who was from one of the wealthiest families in Harlem. Two years later, Johnson wrote *The Autobiography of an Ex-Colored Man*, but he did not publish the book under his own name. Many at the time thought a white man had written the book. The book was largely ignored until it was rediscovered during the Harlem Renaissance. It was reissued in 1927 with Johnson credited as the author.

In the book, Johnson looked at not only the relations between the races but also the problems within the black race. He examined what "blackness" was. The reemergence of the novel gave writers a way to look inward as a way to achieve racial identity. Black writers no longer wanted to focus on just prejudice and bigotry directed at blacks, but they also wanted to explore the psychology of *being* black.[10]

James Weldon Johnson is pictured here meeting with prominent leaders of the National Association of Colored People (NAACP). He encouraged many black writers and artists.

In 1916, Johnson joined the NAACP, where he worked for the next fifteen years. He became the NAACP's first black executive secretary in 1920 and was appointed the chief executive officer in 1931. During the time he worked at the NAACP, he led crusades against disenfranchisement—blacks being denied the right to vote in southern elections.

Throughout his many careers, Johnson continued to write. He completed his first book of poetry, *Fifty Years and Other Poems*, in 1917. Five years later he edited *The Book of American Negro Poetry*. In

1927, Johnson wrote *God's Trombones* with his brother Rosamond. This book was his favorite. It was the result of Johnson's trip to rural Georgia while a college freshman, which had sparked his interest in the African-American folk tradition.[11]

Many of Johnson's poems have been recited in churches all over the world, and his song "Lift Every Voice and Sing" is in many hymnals. Although Johnson is known for his poems of religious beauty, he was actually an agnostic (someone who believes that the existence of God is unknowable and unable to be proved).

Both Johnson and his brother Rosamond knew how to use Negro material for their own prosperity and success. But they also had a plan behind the dialect poetry and minstrel music—it was intended to uplift society. Johnson's writing could move listeners to tears and to careful consideration of "social injustice and moral deficiency."[12]

In 1930, Johnson wrote *Black Manhattan*, a book that discussed the contributions of blacks to the artistic movement in New York. He noted in his book that in the 1920s, Harlem was the "black metropolis" in the heart of a white city and was the capital of black America.[13] He concluded *Black Manhattan* with the hope that the Harlem Renaissance would finally put to rest all racial misconceptions held by white America. But it didn't happen. A year later Johnson abandoned Harlem for Fisk University.

Johnson accepted a position as writer-in-residence at Fisk University in 1931, hoping it would give him more time to write. However, aspiring writers who wanted his advice constantly sought him out. Only the most gifted of hopefuls got even stray notes in the margins of their manuscripts. Most received a polite "nonacceptance" from his secretary.[14] His detached air disappointed Fisk students who were looking forward to working with such an important writer.

While teaching creative literature at Fisk, Johnson wrote his autobiography, *Along This Way.* It was published in 1933. His last book of prose was *Negro Americans, What Now?*, which was published in 1934. Charles S. Johnson (no relation), editor of the National Urban League's magazine *Opportunity*, quoted James Weldon Johnson as saying, "'What shall we do with the Negro?' In asking the question, it completely ignores the fact that the Negro is doing something with himself, and also the equally important fact that the Negro all the while is doing something with America."[15] James Weldon Johnson's last book of poetry, *Selected Poems*, was published in 1936.

Two years later, on June 26, 1938, Johnson was riding in a car in a heavy rainstorm in Wiscasset, Maine, when a train struck the car and Johnson was killed. Over two thousand mourners attended his funeral in Harlem. Johnson was buried in a cemetery in Brooklyn, New York, wearing a lounging robe and holding a copy of his book *God's Trombones* in his hands.

Alain LeRoy Locke

2

Alain LeRoy Locke

(1886–1954)

Some historians have said that no suitable biography of Alain LeRoy Locke could ever be written. They felt that there were no writers who existed who could understand the breadth and depth of Locke's knowledge.[1]

Charles S. Johnson, often called the principal architect of the Harlem Renaissance, said so in a 1954 address at Howard University in Washington, D.C. The occasion was a celebration of the Harlem Renaissance, some three decades earlier. "We are, in a sense, memorializing Alain Locke, an important maker of history who is himself inadequately recorded," Johnson said.[2]

Alain LeRoy Locke was born on September 13, 1886, in Philadelphia, Pennsylvania. He was the only child of two teachers. Locke was brought up in a middle-class home and referred to his family as "smug gentility."[3]

When Alain was a baby, his father died. It was his mother who helped to focus Alain's sights on academic achievement. He was not only a good student but a skilled musician, playing the piano and the violin as well.[4]

At fifteen, Alain graduated from high school. He went on to attend a teacher-training institution. In 1904, he was accepted at Harvard University in Massachusetts, where there were very few black undergraduate students at the time.[5]

Locke graduated in 1907, magna cum laude (with highest honors) with a bachelor of arts degree in philosophy. He was also elected to Phi Beta Kappa, an elite national honor society for college graduates. He was also named the first black Rhodes Scholar, a scholarship given to outstanding students for study abroad.

From 1907 to 1910, Locke studied at Oxford University in England and also spent a year at the University of Berlin, in Germany. In 1911, he returned to the United States for a teaching position at Howard University. He returned to Harvard University for two years and earned his doctorate of philosophy (Ph.D.) in 1918. Except for these two years at Harvard, Locke spent his entire career as head of the philosophy department at Howard University after accepting the position in 1918.[6]

Locke was interested in and had studied African culture and traditions. He was known for his leadership in promoting black culture and black art. During the Harlem Renaissance, he helped the careers of many new young writers and poets, encouraging them to write about black life. He influenced black artists and musicians to look to Africa for both identity and inspiration for their work.

In 1923, Locke began to publish a number of essays in the National Urban League (NUL) magazine *Opportunity*. On March 21, 1924, Charles S. Johnson, editor of *Opportunity*, hosted a dinner at New York City's Civic Club. It was planned as a celebration for the first work of writer Jessie Fauset. The dinner, instead, turned into a major literary event where Johnson introduced the blossoming black literary figures to the white literary establishment.

Paul U. Kellogg, editor of the magazine *The Survey Graphic*, decided to create a special March 1925 issue on the Harlem Renaissance. He asked Locke to be the guest editor and to use the issue as a forum for exposing a white audience to black writers. The special issue was subtitled *Harlem: Mecca of the New Negro*.[7]

Later in 1925, Locke took the special issue and expanded it into a book, this time including critical comment as well as art and literature. Boni & Liveright published Locke's expanded volume as *The New Negro*. Locke used that term to describe a new

Seventh Avenue in Harlem, New York City, as it looked during the Harlem Renaissance.

breed of blacks inside and outside of the arts that had emerged after World War I.[8]

Locke said, "[The] younger generation is vibrant with a new psychology from social disillusionment to race pride." The new mind-set rejected the old stereotypes of black aunties, uncles, and mammies and adopted a psychology of self-respect, self-dependency, and racial unity.[9]

Despite all that Locke did for younger writers, he was disliked by many of them—perhaps because he was thought to have an "uppity" attitude. Only writers Countee Cullen and Langston Hughes expressed

24

any kind of fondness or respect for him. Zora Neale Hurston and Claude McKay, two other writers of the Harlem Renaissance, were especially critical of him, even though Locke had tried to help them both.

Hurston hinted that it had been Charles S. Johnson who had collected the material that Locke had published in *The New Negro*. Possibly, Hurston's feelings toward Locke may have been created because of the harsh review he had given her novel *Their Eyes Were Watching God.*[10]

Other writers accused Locke of changing their work without permission or of being unqualified to provide leadership of the Harlem Renaissance. Many writers believed that Locke played favorites and that he talked badly about other writers behind their backs.

Writer Claude McKay was angry at Locke for changing the title of McKay's poem "The White House" to "White Houses" when it was published in *The New Negro*. Locke had been concerned that readers would take it as a criticism of the president's residence or the man in it. McKay, however, felt that Locke's title implied that McKay disliked all white people.[11]

Locke wanted the Harlem Renaissance to be a purely literary, not political, movement. In "The Negro Takes His Place in American Art," Locke said, "There are . . . three objectives to the movement in Negro Art. . . . One is the encouragement of the Negro artist; another the development of Negro art;

and a third is the promotion of the Negro theme and subject as a vital phase of the artistic expression of American life."[12]

He felt that the subject of race should be used to express art, not to help political causes. Even years after the Harlem Renaissance had waned, Locke noted that when "racial themes are imposed upon the Negro author from within or without, they become an intolerable and limiting artistic ghetto. . . ."[13]

After spending half his life in the field of philosophy, Locke published his first article on philosophy in 1935. By then, the Harlem Renaissance was over and Locke was moving on to other interests.

One of the subjects that interested Locke was the relationship between Africa and African Americans. He believed that a good deal of the connection was seen in the visual arts. Locke became a collector of both African and African-American art, and he encouraged Howard University to enlarge its African art collection.

He also believed in the connection between African music and African-American folk music. He said that black folk music was "almost as important for the musical culture of America as it is for the Negro."[14]

Locke established the Associates in Negro Folk Education, which was dedicated to publishing studies of African-American culture. He wrote several books based on black art and music. *Negro Art: Past and Present* and *The Negro and His Music* were both published in 1936. *The Negro in Art: A Pictorial Record of the Negro Artists and the Negro Theme in Art* were published in 1940.[15]

In 1942, Locke continued his examination of the races, culture, and philosophy. He coedited an anthology on global race relations called *When Peoples Meet: A Study in Race and Culture Contacts.* Many consider this anthology his best work. He was in the process of expanding it and going beyond the original in a volume focused entirely on African-American cultural identity. He worked on it for years.

Unfortunately, he did not live to finish it. Alain LeRoy Locke died on June 9, 1954, in Washington, D.C., from heart disease. The daughter of a colleague at Howard University, Margaret Just Butcher, completed Locke's research and published *The Negro in American Culture.*[16]

In many ways, Alain Locke did more than represent the Harlem Renaissance. He truly was a renaissance man himself.

Zora Neale Hurston

3

Zora Neale Hurston
(1891–1960)

An independent feminist, Zora Neale Hurston was a writer of stories and novels, a playwright, and an anthropologist who was a pioneer in the study of black folklore. She was a trendsetter and lived her life as she chose, in her own style and manner.

Zora Neale Hurston was born in Eatonville, Florida, on January 7, 1891. She was the fifth of eight children born to John Hurston, a carpenter and Baptist preacher, and Lucy Ann Potts, a school-teacher. John Hurston also served as mayor of Eatonville, the first incorporated all-black city.

John and Lucy led a comfortable life in an eight-room house on five acres of land.[1] Although they often argued and John frequently threatened Lucy and the children with physical violence, they stayed together. In her autobiography, *Dust Tracks on a Road*, Hurston did not seem to find physical violence against women and children as alarming as it would be considered today.

The most traumatic event of Zora's childhood occurred when her mother died on September 18, 1904. "That night, all of Mama's children were assembled together for the last time on earth."[2] Zora's brother and sister, Bob and Sarah, returned to school in Jacksonville, Florida. As her father traveled frequently, arrangements were made for nine-year-old Zora, although underage, to be accepted at the same school.

While Zora was away at school, her father remarried. His new wife caused a deep split in the family. Suddenly, Zora's school tuition payments from her family stopped. John Hurston told the school that he was through with Zora and that the school could adopt her if they wished. Zora finished the year by working for the school. She went home briefly but was no longer welcome there.

Hurston completed high school at Morgan Academy in Baltimore, Maryland, in 1918. She tried working as a maid and a governess to earn a living. Then she worked as a waitress in a nightclub and as a manicurist in a black-owned barbershop that served only white clients. One day a black client came in and was refused service. "It was only that night in bed that I analyzed the whole thing and realized that I was giving sanction to Jim Crow [discrimination against blacks], which theoretically, I was supposed to resist."[3] Hurston said.

In 1918, Hurston attended the Howard Prep School in Washington, D.C. A year later she entered Howard University, also in Washington, D.C., and received an associate degree in 1920. She joined *The Stylus* literary society, which she said later greatly influenced the rest of her life. The group was limited to nineteen members, two of whom had to be faculty members. "Dr. Alain LeRoy Locke was the presiding genius. . . ,"[4] Hurston wrote later.

Charles S. Johnson, of the National Urban League (NUL), discovered Hurston because of a short story she had written for *The Stylus*. Johnson asked to see more of her work for his new magazine, *Opportunity*. Hurston sent two of her stories, "Drenched in Light" and "Spunk," which Johnson published.

In January 1925, Hurston decided to move to New York City. She had only $1.50, no job, and no friends, but she had "a lot of hope."[5]

At the *Opportunity* literary awards dinner on May 1, 1925, Hurston received the most honors that night. Out of seven hundred submissions, she won second place for drama for *Color Struck*, second place for fiction for "Spunk," and honorable mention for two other works.[6]

As a result of Hurston's writing success, Annie Nathan Meyer, founder of Barnard College in New York City, offered her a scholarship to the college. In the fall of 1925, Hurston became a student at Barnard. Her adviser recommended that she take some anthropology courses from anthropologist Franz Boas. Two weeks before her graduation in 1928, Boas told Hurston that he had arranged a fellowship for her to study African-American folklore in the South.

On her trip south, Hurston was reunited with her oldest brother, Bob. She learned that their father had been killed in a car accident. Bob also told her the whereabouts of the other Hurston children. "I felt the warm embrace of kin and kind for the first time since the night after my mother's funeral, when we had huddled about the organ all sodden and bewildered, with the walls of our home suddenly blown down."[7]

Hurston moved back to New York City to a rooming house on West 136th Street, which provided rent-free rooms for artists and writers. Hurston called it "Niggerati Manor."[8]

Hurston met Charlotte Mason, a wealthy white patron of artists and writers of the Harlem Renaissance. Mason was providing financial support to the writer Langston Hughes, and she became Hurston's sponsor as well. She paid Hurston two hundred dollars a month for two years to write and conduct her folklore research, which then became Mason's property. In addition to the financial support, Mason gave Hurston the advice and spiritual guidance she had missed since her mother died.[9]

In 1927, Hurston and Langston Hughes were in Mobile, Alabama. They began to collaborate on a "Negro opera" (a play), as a way to join the Talented Tenth (the elite of the black community) and the Niggerati (black writers and artists).[10] In 1930, Charlotte Mason rented a house for them in Westfield, New Jersey, to finish their play.

Mason had Alain Locke check on their progress. When he reported that there was not enough serious work taking place, Mason was displeased. Hurston then decided to leave and she headed south, with only the first and third acts of the play completed.

It was the beginning of the end of the relationship. Hughes barely spoke to Hurston, Locke, or Mason ever again. Then Hurston copyrighted the play under her name as sole author, calling it *Mule Bone*. (It was finally produced in 1991 at New York City's Lincoln Center for the Arts.[11])

Hurston never published any books while under Mason's protective censorship. In 1929, Hurston got the idea for her book *Jonah's Gourd Vine*. She resisted writing it at first, feeling pressure as a black woman to write about race only. ". . . Negroes were supposed to write about the Race Problem. I was and am thoroughly sick of the subject," she said.[12]

By May 1932, Hurston had lost most of her money in the Great Depression. She decided to publish some of her anthropological studies, which Charlotte Mason had not allowed her to do previously. Hurston also gave some concerts of folk songs she had collected and

Hurston published five books of dreams, stories, and essays. The first book was called *Mules and Men*, a collection of seventy stories.

wrote a story, "The Gilded Six-Bits." After one professor read the story to his creative writing class, he sent it to *Story Magazine*, which published it in August 1933. As a result of its publication, four publishers wrote to Hurston and asked if she had any book-length work. Based on their correspondence, she began to work on *Jonah's Gourd Vine* for the J. B. Lippincott Company.

In the mid-1930s, Hurston produced five books of drama, stories, and essays. She published her first book, *Mules and Men*, which was her anthropological research presented as a collection of seventy stories.

During her travels, often abroad, Hurston continued to write. She returned to the United States from a trip to Haiti after having written her book *Their Eyes Were Watching God* in seven weeks' time.[13] It was published in 1937, and it is widely considered to be her best work.

Only two more books of Hurston's were published in the next twenty years before her death. Her "charming and unreliable autobiography,"[14] *Dust Tracks on a Road*, was published in 1942. Her last book, *Seraph on the Suwanee*, was published in 1948 and received positive reviews.

Hurston continued to publish essays such as "What White Publishers Won't Print" and "I Saw Negro Votes Peddled," but she was unable to support herself from her writing. Hurston returned to Florida and worked at a number of jobs. While working as a maid, her essay "Conscience of the Court" was published in the *Saturday Evening Post* magazine.[15]

Hurston suffered a stroke in early 1959 and had to go to the St. Lucie County Welfare Home in October.[16] She died on January 28, 1960, of heart disease and was buried in an unmarked grave in the Garden of Heaven Rest cemetery in Fort Pierce, Florida.

Novelist Alice Walker discovered Hurston's grave in August 1973 and arranged for a grave marker. In March 1975, Walker published "In Search of Zora Neale Hurston" in *Ms.* magazine, which raised interest in Hurston's life and works. Walker put on Hurston's grave marker a line from a Jean Toomer poem: "Zora Neale Hurston: 'A Genius of the South.'"[17]

Bessie Smith
(1894?–1937)

Bessie Smith was a larger-than-life force. Self-assured, independent, and confident of her talent, she became a black cultural symbol and a legend in her own time. She attracted both black and white audiences with her strong voice and powerful personality.

Bessie Smith was born in Chattanooga, Tennessee. Her birth date is not certain, but is most commonly thought to be April 15, 1894. (Some sources cite 1895, 1896, 1898, and 1900.) She was one of seven children. Her father, William, was an unskilled laborer and part-time Baptist minister.[1] Her mother, Laura, and her father both died when Bessie was young. She was raised by her sister Viola, who supported the family by taking in white people's laundry.

Bessie Smith

Bessie's brother Clarence was an entertainer and encouraged her to learn to sing and dance. Even as early as nine years old, Bessie was singing for money. After Clarence joined a traveling vaudeville show, Bessie and another brother, Andrew, began singing to earn money from people on the street.[2]

Clarence arranged for an audition with the Moses Stokes Company, the company he had been touring with.[3] In her teens, Smith began performing as a singer and dancer with small-time tent shows such as Charles P. Bailey's troupe and Pete Werley's Florida Cotton Blossoms.[4] It soon became clear that Smith was a better singer than a dancer. Starting out in the chorus, she worked her way up to featured singer.

Around 1912, Smith performed mostly in carnivals, theaters, and tents with Pa and Ma Rainey and other traveling shows. Ma Rainey was called the Mother of the Blues.[5] There is little doubt that Ma Rainey probably influenced Smith and helped her learn her craft. Rainey's keen sense of interpretation and phrasing influenced most of the female blues artists that came after her.[6]

Bessie Smith was an unusual character. She was about six feet tall, weighed over two hundred pounds, was bisexual, an alcoholic, and had a very foul mouth. She was tough. Nobody wanted to mess with Bessie Smith.

She was married twice, the first time to Earl Love, who died shortly after they were married. Her second husband was Jack Gee. He was a security guard. Both Gee and Smith were strong and violent people, and their marriage was stormy. They often got into knockdown, drag-out fights.[7]

During World War I, Smith created a show called *Liberty Belles*. Although audiences loved it, theater managers would not book it. The reason might have been because of its raunchy material.

Smith moved to Philadelphia, Pennsylvania, in 1921. She auditioned for Okeh Records but her voice was considered "too rough" to make records. Two years later, in 1923, Smith signed with Columbia Records. For $125 and no royalties, she recorded "Down-Hearted Blues" and "Gulf Coast Blues," accompanied by Clarence Williams on the piano. Her two debut songs became instant hits and sold 780,000 copies in six months. By the end of the first year, her records had sold over 2 million copies.[8]

In the next eight years, no other record on the Columbia label sold more copies. Unfortunately, because of a bad contract, Smith received only $28,575 from these two hits.[9] After that, Smith was careful with her contracts so as not to be exploited like that again.

Bessie Smith became known as the Empress of the Blues. From 1923 to 1933, Smith recorded more than 150 songs for Columbia. At her peak, she earned over $2,000 a week, which was an enormous amount of money in the 1920s.[10]

Smith recorded with some of the great blues and jazz legends, including pianist Fletcher Henderson, cornet and trumpet player Louis Armstrong, and clarinetist Buster Bailey. Many of her early songs were recorded with piano accompaniment alone, which helped focus attention on her vocal style and delivery. Armstrong said of Smith, "She used to thrill me at all times, the way she could phrase a note with a certain something in her voice no other blues singer could get."[11]

Smith composed a lot of her music, although she could barely read. She learned the lyrics as they were read to her. Two of the songs she composed became blues classics: "Back Water Blues" and "Poor Man's Blues." For Smith, "the blues" music was her way to communicate the black experience. Poet Langston Hughes described Smith as "not softened with tears, but hardened with laughter, the absurd, incongruous laughter of a sadness without even a god to appeal to."[12]

Smith's songs tell a lot about the black culture. Many African Americans felt that she was a hero of sorts, having triumphed over the whites who dominated the entertainment industry. Two of her recordings with jazz musician, Louis Armstrong, are pure classics: "You've Been a Good Ole Wagon" and "St. Louis Blues." The latter was recorded January 14, 1925. In addition to twenty-four-year-old Armstrong, Smith was also accompanied by Fred Longshaw on the reed organ.[13]

41

Bessie Smith was the highest-paid African-American female singer during her peak in the 1920s.

Smith had some very successful tours in the 1920s. She performed mostly in all-black theaters in the Deep South, so whites knew her mainly through her recordings. Smith made it to Broadway for three performances of a play called *Pansy* in 1929, before it flopped.[14]

She recorded the prophetic song "Nobody Knows You When You're Down and Out" in 1929. Historian William Barlow called this song her "personal epitaph and a depression-era classic."[15]

By 1931, the blues had gone out of style for recording. Record companies began to have trouble selling records because of the Great Depression, radio, and movies with sound. People no longer wanted to buy records when they could listen to free music on radio broadcasts.

Columbia Records dropped Bessie Smith as a recording artist. Her last recording was in 1933. It was made under the direction of talent scout John Hammond for Okeh. White musicians Jack Teagarden (on the trombone) and Benny Goodman (on the clarinet) played in the sessions.[16]

Despite the lack of a recording label, Smith still continued to pull in large crowds in her tours in the South. However, she did not make nearly as much money as she had during the 1920s, when she was the highest-paid African-American female singer. The rough-cut sound of the blues had yielded to the smoother, more polished tones of swing. Smith's heavy gin drinking, begun when she was just a teenager, started to take a toll on her voice and her performance. She last performed in New York in 1936 at the Famous Door on Fifty-second Street. It was a jam session sponsored by the United Hot Clubs of America.[17]

In 1937, Smith was transforming her style from classical blues to swing, and was on the verge of a comeback, when disaster struck. She and her boyfriend, Richard Morgan, were driving when Smith's car hit a slow-moving truck. Their car rolled over, breaking Smith's ribs. Her right arm was so badly crushed it was almost severed. Smith bled to death before she reached a hospital.

John Hammond, interviewed for an article for *Downbeat* magazine, said that a hospital nearby would not allow a black to be treated there. Hammond went on to say that Smith bled to death while being transported to a hospital that would accept blacks.[18] Later, Hammond admitted that his remarks were based on hearsay and rumor. The playwright Edward Albee wrote *The Death of Bessie Smith* based on the rumors about her death.

What is true is that Bessie Smith died on September 26, 1937, at the Afro-American Hospital in Clarksdale, Mississippi. Her death was a result of her injuries from the car accident. She was forty-three years old. Smith was buried at Mount Lawn Cemetery in Philadelphia. In 1970, a tombstone was erected on Smith's grave. It says: "The greatest blues singer in the world will never stop singing."[19]

There are few opportunities for today's audiences to hear Bessie Smith. However, in 1929, she did perform in a short film called *The St. Louis Blues*, but it is rare footage, and viewings are not readily available.

Unlike singers Billie Holiday and Josephine Baker of the same era, there have been no major biographical features on Bessie Smith's life for stage or screen. But her talent and achievement were acknowledged when she was inducted into the Blues Foundation's Hall of Fame in 1980, the Rock & Roll Hall of Fame in 1989, and the National Women's Hall of Fame in 1998.[20]

Aaron Douglas

5

Aaron Douglas
(1898–1979)

Aaron Douglas was the best known and the most popular artist of the Harlem Renaissance. His work expressed both the heritage and culture of African Americans. His striking illustrations graced the covers of books and magazines, as well as the walls of buildings. He was considered the father of African-American art.

Aaron Douglas was born May 26, 1898, in Topeka, Kansas. Early on, he displayed an aptitude and interest in art, and he decided to became an artist. He was influenced strongly by the work of African-American painter Henry Ossawa Tanner, whom he greatly admired.

Douglas attended the University of Nebraska in Lincoln, following his service in World War I. He received a bachelor of arts degree in fine arts in 1922. After teaching drawing at a high school in Kansas City, Kansas, Douglas decided to move to New York City to become part of the Harlem Renaissance movement. Years later, Douglas said that he was impressed at seeing a city that was "entirely black, from beginning to end you were impressed by the fact that black people were in charge of things and here was a black city and here was a situation that was eventually to be the center for the great in American Culture."[1]

In New York, Douglas's artwork changed from the style of his work in Kansas. His emphasis there had been on the traditional art of an academic environment. Now it was replaced by a style known as cubism,[2] where natural forms are broken into simple geometric shapes, such as rectangles, circles, and triangles.

Winold Reiss, a white German illustrator from Bavaria, who painted portraits of many Harlem Renaissance artists and writers, befriended Douglas. Reiss encouraged Douglas to look to African art for inspiration for his work, and Douglas became strongly influenced by African folk culture and design.

Douglas's style is most easily recognized by his use of silhouettes, hard geometric edges, pictures of African history, and angular rays of light. In a letter to poet Langston Hughes, Douglas described what he wanted to accomplish with his work: "Your problem, Langston, my problem, no our problem is to conceive, develop, establish an art era. Not white art painted black. . . . Let's do the impossible. Let's create something transcendentally material, mystically objective. Earthy. Spiritually earthy. Dynamic."[3]

Douglas's art caught the eye of W. E. B. Du Bois, a founder of the National Association for the Advancement of Colored People (NAACP). Du Bois and author Alain Locke had been trying to encourage African-American artists to express their African heritage in their artwork.

Douglas was asked to illustrate a number of works by African-American writers. As a result of his work and influence, Douglas became known as the Dean of African-American painters, which was also a title given to artist Henry Ossawa Tanner,[4] the artist whose work had influenced Douglas in his early career.

In 1924, Alain Locke commissioned Douglas to create drawings for Locke's anthology of black writers, *The New Negro*. Douglas's most famous illustrations, however, were for James Weldon Johnson's 1927 book, *God's Trombones: Seven Sermons in Verse*.

Charles S. Johnson, editor of the National Urban League (NUL) magazine, *Opportunity*, encouraged Douglas to move to Harlem. Thanks partly to his friendship with Johnson, Douglas received a Barnes

Foundation fellowship, as well as another fellowship for independent study at the Academie Scandinave in Paris, France.[5]

Like many others active in the Harlem Renaissance, Douglas was sponsored by Charlotte Mason. She was a wealthy white patron interested in supporting the creative talents of African-American writers and artists. She offered them financial assistance, which gave them the freedom to concentrate their creative energies on their work.

Historian David Levering Lewis notes that the Harlem Renaissance arts movement had a superficiality. It was as if the whites and other people of influence were saying: "We perceive that you have something that can be parlayed into some form of expression." For example, the NAACP set out "systematically to entice African Americans of all careers to become 'artists.'"[6]

Du Bois of the NAACP had hoped to persuade artist Henry O. Tanner, who was living in Europe at the time, to return to the United States to create an art school for African Americans.

Douglas called this the "vacuum cleaner approach to art," where any "poor fool caught with a brush in his hand" was turned into an artist. As a result, barely talented and even untalented black artists were put on display and praised for mediocre works.[7]

What emerged was a sense of urgency in the arts. Douglas explained, "[We] were so hungry at that time for something that was specifically black that they were perfectly willing to accept almost anything. I say that because as I look back at the things that I produced, it was so readily received and cheerfully received. You wonder how they could have done it! I look at it and I wonder how I could have done it. And next, could there have been a group to receive it, who were willing to receive it?"[8]

In 1926, writer Wallace Thurman and a group of six other literary members of the Harlem Renaissance gathered their considerable talents with the intent of publishing their own cutting-edge magazine. Wallace Thurman, poet Langston Hughes, and writer Zora Neale Hurston were part of what was considered the "inner circle" of the young Harlem Renaissance. They dictated the style and pace that characterized the black creative movement.

Thurman and the others wanted to offer another publishing outlet besides the very conservative publications of the NAACP and NUL, *The Crisis* and *Opportunity*. They called their magazine *Fire!! (A Quarterly Devoted to the Younger Negro Artists)*.

In addition to being listed as an editor, Douglas created the cover for *Fire!!*, with a primitive black design and red print. The inside illustrations continued the African theme with jungle scenes and various nude figures.[9]

Aaron Douglas (left) discusses the *Aspects of Negro Life: Song of the Towers* series with Arthur Schomburg. Each mural in the series depicts African-American life and culture.

Fire!! was published only once, in November 1926. The magazine had both financial and distribution problems, and it did not survive beyond the first issue. Many of the seven contributing writers had sunk their savings into the magazine, especially editor Thurman. Ironically, the many unsold issues of *Fire!!* were lost when the house in which they were stored burned down.

In 1927, Douglas began to take on larger tasks. He became president of the Harlem Artists Guild. He created illustrations for *The Crisis* and *Opportunity* magazines, relying heavily on African art for inspiration, especially that of Egypt. One of his larger works was a set of murals he painted in 1929 for the College Inn Ballroom in the Sherman Hotel in Chicago. Another mural, created in 1930, was at Fisk University, in Nashville, Tennessee.[10]

In 1934, Douglas was given a commission to paint a series of murals for the 135th Street Branch of the New York Public Library.[11] The murals were called *Aspects of Negro Life*. There were four panels representing the cultural and historical African heritage of African Americans. The panels showed scenes of African music and dance; slavery, emancipation, and the Reconstruction periods; mass migration of blacks to the industrial North; the Harlem Renaissance; and the Great Depression.

Douglas left Harlem in 1937 for Fisk University and founded the art department there. As part of the art program, Douglas had his students study black history, which he felt was important to understanding art. While at the university, Douglas created a mural for the Erastus Milo Cravath Memorial Library at Fisk, which is considered his best work.[12]

Aaron Douglas retired in 1966 as head of the art department at Fisk. However, he continued to paint and give lectures until his death on February 3, 1979.

6

Duke Ellington
(1899–1974)

Sophisticated, elegant, gifted as a musician, composer, and bandleader, Edward Kennedy Ellington achieved world fame in his lifetime. The many awards, honors, and degrees he received were acknowledgment of the major contributions he made to the world of music.

Edward Kennedy Ellington was born on April 29, 1899, in Washington, D.C. His parents, Daisy Kennedy Ellington and James Edward Ellington, also had a daughter, Ruth, who became the longtime steward of Ellington's work.[1]

Edward was nicknamed "Duke" by his friends because even as a child he took pride in his clothes and appearance. When he became an adult, his elegant

Edward Kennedy Ellington, "Duke Ellington."

clothes became his trademark. No other performer wore white tails on stage until Ellington did.[2]

Duke Ellington grew up in Washington, D.C., in a middle-class African-American community. He began studying piano around the age of seven and received formal music instruction. Duke studied harmony with Henry Grant at Armstrong High School.[3] He made his professional debut at the age of seventeen playing at local social events.

Duke was also interested in art and liked to paint and draw. But he decided to make music his career. Despite his classical music training, he was attracted to a more "common" type of black music. He started hanging out in poolrooms and nightclubs to listen to the music of ragtime pianists and composers.

On July 2, 1918, at the age of twenty-four, Ellington married his high school sweetheart, Edna Thompson. Their only child, Mercer, was born the following year. Jazz pianist Fats Waller encouraged Ellington to move to New York City, which he did in 1923, with his wife and son.

In 1923, Ellington formed his first band, the six-member band called the Washingtonians, and played at the Hollywood Club. Ellington made his first record in 1924. The band recorded under different names—The Jungle Band, The Whoopee Makers, and The Harlem Footwarmers.[4] Ellington and his band became part of the music scene in New York.

In this era, bandleaders did much more than just write music and lead the band. Ellington, for example, also managed the group, did its bookings and travel arrangements, and carried out public-relations activities as well.[5]

Ellington's band auditioned at Harlem's Cotton Club and was hired. They were the houseband from 1927 to 1930. The Cotton Club was one of the most famous nightclubs in New York in the 1920s and 1930s. It was a whites-only nightclub but featured the most famous black performers of the day. White patrons from downtown New York City took the A train up to Harlem to visit the speakeasies. (Speakeasies were places, such as clubs, where alcohol was sold during the Prohibition period, when it was unlawful to sell liquor.)

The Cotton Club was opened in 1923 by Owney Madden and "Big Frenchy" de Mange. It was the largest of the Harlem nightclubs that served white audiences exclusively. It had the most extravagant shows, charged the highest prices, and strictly enforced the rules excluding black patrons. Madden opened the club so he could sell his illegal liquor—waiters told customers to keep their bottles of bootleg liquor in their pockets and not place them on the floor.[6]

The Cotton Club's shows, featuring Ellington's big-band jazz, ran up to two hours and featured both a special act, such as a comedian, and the regular performers. The regular performers included the Cotton Club's band (wearing tuxedos) and the Cotton Club's famous "sepia" chorus line of girl dancers. Girls with sepia (light brown) skin color were considered more presentable to white audiences.

Besides the club's double standard of having black performers but allowing only white patrons in the club, there was a subtler double standard. Although the chorus girls had to be what was called "high yaller" to work there, it did not matter what the skin color was of the male dancers, which ranged from light brown to very dark. Ellington's composition, "Black and Tan Fantasy," referred to this double-color standard of the club.[7]

Ellington's popularity, along with that of black entertainers, such as singer Bessie Smith and dancer Bill "Bojangles" Robinson, went beyond the Harlem Renaissance. "[It] is impossible to imagine American music without them," said historian Dr. Steven Watson.[8]

Duke Ellington wrote a few songs in the 1920s, but most of his successful musical compositions came after the Harlem Renaissance. Two of his best-loved hits were "Mood Indigo" (1930) and "Sophisticated Lady" (1933). His most famous title, which summarized much of the music of the Harlem Renaissance and the jazz era was "It Don't Mean a Thing (If It Ain't Got That Swing)" (1932).[9]

However, Ellington's band was not just a swing band. He experimented with different sounds and gave his music "a new feeling with his special effects, using instruments in new ways, and infusing African and Latin elements into his music."[10]

In addition to directing and composing, Duke Ellington managed, made bookings, travel arrangements, and carried out public relations activities. Here Duke Ellington speaks with students at Boston University in 1955.

By the 1930s, Ellington had become a recognized leader in orchestral composition. When his mother died in 1935, Ellington composed a piece in her memory, called *Reminiscing in Tempo*.[11]

Ellington created his publishing company, Tempo Music, in 1941, with his sister as its executive leader. Ruth Ellington had graduated from Columbia University, intending to become a doctor. Instead, she became the caretaker of the Ellington musical empire.

In his autobiography, *Music Is My Mistress*, Ellington wrote: "Ruth's upbringing and education equipped her as a gentlewoman and were not designed to develop aggressive or businesslike qualities. She operates Tempo Music as though it were a publishing house of classical music rather than of jazz . . . and she is more concerned with its prestige than its profitability."[12]

Throughout the 1940s, Ellington and his band appeared in a number of movie musicals such as *Black and Tan Fantasy* and the Marx Brothers' *A Day at the Races*. He also composed the music for many other movies in which he did not appear.

In 1951, Ellington created *Harlem*, a major piece that premiered at a National Association for the Advancement of Colored People (NAACP) fundraiser. Ellington wrote a letter to President Harry S. Truman, saying the concert would benefit "your civil rights program to stamp out segregation, discrimination [and] bigotry."[13]

By the mid-1950s, bcbop and then rock 'n' roll music had passed swing and jazz in popularity. Although swing bands seemed like dinosaurs—too big, too old, too slow—Ellington's band still survived and thrived. He even made the cover of *Time* magazine in 1956.

In the 1960s, Ellington collaborated with the Count Basie orchestra and the Louis Armstrong All Stars. In addition, he worked with younger recording artists and cut several record albums. Ellington also wrote *My People*, celebrating the one hundredth anniversary of the Emancipation Proclamation.[14]

Young civil rights activists, who had not been around during the Harlem Renaissance, criticized Ellington for not getting more involved in the movement. Ellington shrugged off their harsh words, knowing that he had done his part in his time.

For his work, Ellington was honored many times during his lifetime. In 1966, President Lyndon Baines Johnson awarded him the Gold Medal of Honor. Ellington also received the Medal of Freedom at President Richard Nixon's birthday festivities in 1969.[15]

Altogether, Ellington received sixteen honorary doctorates from American universities—including Howard and Yale—as well as the French Legion of Honor, membership in the American Institute of Arts and Letters, and election as the first jazz musician member of the Royal Music Academy in Stockholm.[16]

Ellington was a devout man, as well, and wrote *Three Sacred Pieces* in the 1960s. He considered these sacred concerts his most important work. Through them, he said that love was interchangeable with his personal conception of God.[17]

Duke Ellington's last concert was performed at Westminster Abbey in London, England, in 1974. He died that year on May 24, at the age of seventy-five. He had written over three hundred songs and composed over one thousand orchestral pieces, including *Black, Brown, and Beige: A Tone Parallel to the History of the Negro in America.*[18]

Mercer Ellington took over the band after his father's death. Two of Mercer's children, daughter Mercedes and son Paul, remained especially active in carrying on the Ellington legacy. Paul assumed leadership of the Duke Ellington Orchestra in 1996 after his father's death.

Langston Hughes

7

Langston Hughes
(1902–1967)

A prolific and versatile writer, Langston Hughes wrote about ordinary African Americans. He was an innovator, experimenting with both form and style, often using dialect and jazz rhythms to portray life in the black culture. He was a major creative force in the Harlem Renaissance.

James Langston Hughes was born in Joplin, Missouri, on February 1, 1902. He was part African American, part French European, and part Cherokee. His father, James Nathaniel Hughes, trained to be a lawyer, but as a black man, he was denied a fair opportunity to practice law. Instead, he went to work for the Lincoln Mining Company in Joplin. However, because of marital problems and racial discrimination, James Hughes left his family and moved to Mexico.

Langston and his mother, Carolina Mercer Langston, moved to Topeka, Kansas, where Carrie Langston petitioned the school board to allow Langston to enroll in the all-white neighborhood school. Although one of Langston's teachers often made racist remarks to him, other teachers and many students befriended him.

"I learned early not to hate *all* white people," said Hughes. "It has seemed to me that *most* people are generally good, in every race and in every country where I have been."[1]

After first grade, Langston lived with his grandmother. When he was twelve, she died and he moved in with an aunt and uncle. Two years later, Langston joined his mother and her new husband, Homer Clark.

In Langston's senior year, his father took him back to Mexico. They had not seen each other since Langston was five years old. Before they had even crossed the border, James Hughes made many negative comments about African Americans. Langston Hughes later wrote, "My father hated Negroes. I think he hated himself, too, for being a Negro."[2]

Langston and his father settled in Mexico City, but it was not a happy relationship. "That summer in Mexico was the most miserable I have ever known," Hughes later said.[3] Langston worked all summer and became sick from physical labor and stress. In August 1919, he returned to school in Cleveland, Ohio.

At Central High School, Langston was nominated for class president but did not win. He acted in the school's drama program, was named class poet and yearbook editor, and wrote and published the school's newspaper.

Langston graduated with honors in June 1920, and knew he wanted to be a writer. He wanted to write about African Americans and black culture. To do this, he felt he needed to immerse himself in an African-American community. He decided to go to New York City and attend Columbia University. But first he decided to smooth things over with his father in Toluca, Mexico.

One evening on the train trip to Mexico, Langston saw the Mississippi River. He was struck by the thought that the river, and other rivers such as the Congo and the Niger, played a part in slavery. Boats carried slaves to places where they would be sold. Right then he sat down and wrote his poem "The Negro Speaks of Rivers."

In Mexico, although Langston and his father started off on better terms, they soon began to argue. Langston noted later that he always wrote best when he felt the worst; when he was happy, he didn't write. In his book *The Big Sea*, he said, "That summer in Mexico, I wrote a great many poems, because I was very unhappy."[4]

James Hughes wanted his son to go to Europe to become a mining engineer, as he had. Langston, however, was unwilling to abandon his dream of going to Harlem and becoming a writer. Finally, an article about Toluca, another about the Virgin of Guadaloupe, and a children's play called *The Gold Piece* were published in *The Brownie's Book*, a magazine founded by W.E.B. Du Bois and edited by writer Jessie Fauset.

Fauset requested more of Hughes's writing and was soon publishing Hughes's work in every issue. Then Hughes sent her "The Negro Speaks of Rivers," which appeared in Du Bois's other magazine, *The Crisis*. It was Hughes's first published poem.

Hughes was not paid for any of these pieces, which was acceptable to him. He was just pleased that he was being published. His father, however, harassed him about it, but agreed to pay for Langston to attend one year at Columbia University in New York City.

At Columbia, Hughes was again made aware of the color barrier. The school paper, *Spectator*, snubbed him, and the editor assigned Hughes to the fraternity and society news. This was a cruel joke, since the events the social reporter covered were closed to an African American.

Hughes became increasingly frustrated at Columbia. After meeting the staff of *The Crisis*, he decided that he needed the kind of education that could be found only among people, not in university halls. He left Columbia and began working odd jobs.

While working on a freighter in the Hudson River, Hughes wrote "The Weary Blues," a poem about a Harlem piano player. When the ship sailed to Africa, Hughes met a color barrier of a different type: He was not considered black, because he was of mixed race. His copper-colored skin and straight black hair identified him as an outsider.

"You see, unfortunately, I am not black," said Hughes in his first autobiography, *The Big Sea*. "[In] the United States, the word 'Negro' is used to mean anyone who has *any* Negro blood at all in his veins. In Africa, the word is more pure. It means *all* Negro, therefore *black*. I am brown."[5]

Hughes made his way to Paris and became an assistant cook at the Grand Duc nightclub. When the Grand Duc closed for August, Hughes toured Italy. A pickpocket took Hughes's money and passport on a train, and he could not reenter France. In this desperate period of his life, he wrote one of his most famous poems: "I, Too."

A merchant vessel with an all-black crew put into port and Hughes got working passage back home in November 1924. Hughes arrived in the United States without a place to live, so he moved in with his mother and stepbrother in Washington, D.C. He hoped to attend Howard University to get a better background for his writing. He took menial jobs to pay his portion of the household expenses.

"I felt very bad in Washington that winter, so I wrote a great many poems," said Hughes.[6] Then came his lucky break. *Opportunity*, the magazine of the National Urban League (NUL), announced a contest for African-American writers. Langston received first place in poetry for his jazzlike "The Weary Blues."

Attending the awards banquet that evening was best-selling novelist Carl Van Vechten. Although white, Van Vechten played an important role in the Harlem Renaissance. He was a serious student of African-American culture, and he and Hughes became friends.

Van Vechten asked Hughes if he had enough work to fill a book. Within days, Van Vechten had Hughes's manuscript and obtained a publishing contract with his own publisher, Alfred A. Knopf. Van Vechten also sold some of Hughes's poems to *Vanity Fair* magazine.

Despite this meteoric rise in his career, Hughes still had to earn a living—so he worked as a busboy at the Wardman Park Hotel in Washington. A famous poet, Vachel Lindsay, was a guest of the hotel to give a poetry reading. Hughes slipped him a note and three poems: "Jazzonia," "Negro Dancers," and "The Weary Blues." Lindsay, impressed with Hughes's talent, read Hughes's poems to the audience.

A month later, Hughes's book of poetry, *The Weary Blues*, was published by Knopf. Soon Hughes was besieged with invitations to read his work.

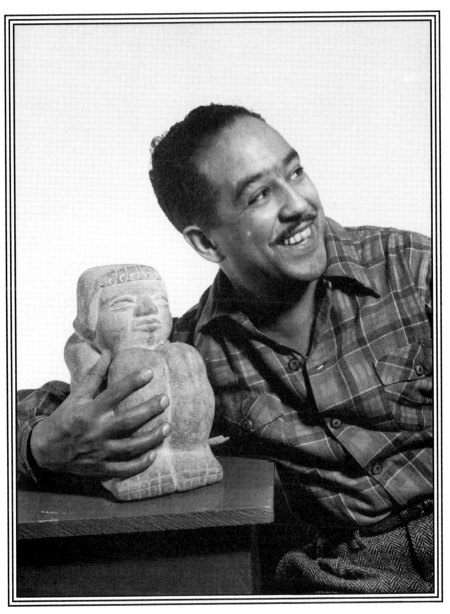

Langston Hughes's poetry and stories appealed to all because he wrote about ordinary African Americans.

In the fall of 1926, Hughes compiled a new group of poems and submitted it to Knopf. The collection, *Fine Clothes to the Jew*, is considered today to be Hughes's greatest achievement. Hughes wrote it in blues style, using African-American dialect in its most poetic form.

The book was published in 1927 to critical outrage from fellow African Americans. Many felt that it romanticized the lower class of African Americans and they thought it was trash. Even the title was heavily criticized. Hughes got the title of the book from the practice of taking clothes to the pawnbroker (who was often Jewish) for quick money. Hughes intended the title to reflect the desperation of the impoverished, but many people were offended. The Chicago *Whip* called Hughes "The Poet Lowrate of Harlem."[7]

Hughes understood the reaction but had not anticipated it: "The Negro critics and many of the intellectuals were very sensitive about their race in books. . . . In anything that white people were likely to read, they wanted to put their best foot forward, their politely polished and cultural foot—and only that foot."[8]

Despite the waning of the Harlem Renaissance, Hughes continued his prolific writing and traveling. He wrote two autobiographies, *The Big Sea* and *I Wonder as I Wander*, as well as other prose. In the 1950s, Hughes began to write for the next generation, producing books about African-American musicians and heroes, in addition to books about his travels.

During his lifetime, Hughes won many awards, honorary degrees, fellowships, and grants. Despite all these honors, none of Hughes's work ever became a best-seller or a smash Broadway hit.

One night in 1967, Hughes awoke in pain and went to the Polyclinic Hospital in Manhattan. His condition unexpectedly deteriorated rapidly, and he died on May 22, 1967, at the age of sixty-five.

Arna Bontemps

8

Arna Bontemps
(1902–1973)

The Harlem Renaissance helped to change the history and image of African Americans. Black culture burst into life during the 1920s and 1930s through the collective talents of African-American artists, writers, musicians, and performers. Black and white audiences were exposed to this cultural revolution, which was both a literary and political movement. Arna Bontemps was there to record for history this exciting and intensely creative period of black life from a black perspective.

Arnaud Wendell Bontemps was born in Alexandria, Louisiana, on October 13, 1902. Arna's parents were Paul Bismarck Bontemps and Maria Pembroke Bontemps. As a result of several racist incidents, Paul Bontemps, a brick mason, moved his family to the Watts section of Los Angeles in 1905, just three days before the great San Francisco earthquake in California.[1]

Arna's parents sent him first to public, then to private schools. Tension arose between Arna and his father when Arna refused to be apprenticed as a mason. Paul Bontemps sent Arna away to a white boarding school in the San Fernando Valley and instructed his son not to "go up there acting colored."[2]

In 1923, Bontemps graduated from Pacific Union College in Angwin, California, with a bachelor of arts degree. While still in college, he became interested in writing. His first poem, "Hope," was published in 1917 in *The Crisis,* the publication of the National Association for the Advancement of Colored People (NAACP). A poem, "A Black Man Talks of Reaping," received a poetry prize in 1926 from *The Crisis.*[3] Also in 1926, another poem,"Golgotha Is a Mountain," won first prize in poetry at the second awards dinner sponsored by the National Urban League's (NUL) magazine, *Opportunity.*[4]

Arna Bontemps married Alberta Johnson, a native of Georgia, and they had six children. Bontemps had hoped to earn his doctorate in philosophy (Ph.D.). He found, however, that after his 1926 marriage he needed to support his growing family, which would be difficult to do if he was in graduate school.

Writer Langston Hughes, a close friend and collaborator, noted in his autobiography, *The Big Sea,* that no one in their circle ever saw Bontemps's

Arna Bontemps and Langston Hughes are sitting with Bontemps's family. Bontemps was working on a novel of Hughes's life before he died in 1973.

wife. "She remained the mystery of the New Negro Renaissance," said Hughes. "But I went with [Bontemps] once to his apartment to meet her, and found her a shy and charming girl, holding a golden baby on her lap . . . And every time I went away . . . and came back, there would be a new golden baby, each prettier than the last—so that was why the literati never saw Mrs. Bontemps."[5]

Bontemps came to Harlem during the second phase of the Renaissance. History professor Cary Wintz noted that Bontemps's greatest contribution to the New Negro Renaissance was not his original literature, but in his role as the "semiofficial historian" of the movement. Bontemps himself stated that he had observed the Renaissance "from a grandstand seat."[6] Arna Bontemps was considered the leading authority on the Harlem Renaissance.

Bontemps was deeply influenced by his culture's black folk traditions, yet he was also affected by the classic traditions of English poetry. The major themes of his writing were historical. From 1924 to 1931, Bontemps wrote essays, short stories, and over twenty fiction, nonfiction, and children's books. He also taught at the Harlem Academy, a private school in New York City.[7]

In 1931, Bontemps left the Harlem Academy to teach at Oakwood Junior College in Huntsville, Alabama.[8] Bontemps's writing was influenced by his Louisiana roots. Now, returning to the South as an adult, he found that some of the old Jim Crow segregation (discrimination against blacks) was changing.

During the 1930s, Bontemps published six books, including one for children called *Sad Face Boy*. Bontemps's 1933 story, "A Summer Tragedy," was the basis for the 1996 short film and Academy Award nominee, *A Tuesday Morning Ride*. A play, *St. Louis Woman*, that Bontemps wrote with Harlem Renaissance writer Countee Cullen, was based on Bontemps's first novel, *God Sends Sunday*. This novel, more than his later two books, reflected the literary themes of the Harlem Renaissance.

Bontemps's 1934 novel, *Black Thunder*, was one of the few historical novels of the Harlem Renaissance. It was based on the Gabriel Prosser slave revolt in

Virginia in 1800.[9] Bontemps also wrote *Drums at Dusk* about another slave revolt in the nineteenth century that took place in Haiti. It was published in 1939.

Bontemps entered the University of Chicago's graduate school to study library science. He received a master's degree in library science in 1943.[10] Bontemps then was appointed head librarian at Fisk University in Nashville, Tennessee.

In the mid-1940s, Bontemps began to focus on writing biographical works. In 1945, he published *We Have Tomorrow*, a collective biography of young African Americans. He also collaborated with Irish-American writer Jack Conroy to write a study of black migration called *They Seek a City*. This book was later expanded and revised in 1966 and reissued as *Anyplace But Here*.

In addition, Bontemps also wrote biographies of scientist George Washington Carver, abolitionist Frederick Douglass, and educator Booker T. Washington.[11] During this period, Bontemps's *Story of the Negro* was chosen as a 1949 Newbery Honor Book, a designation awarded to outstanding American literature for children. In 1956, Bontemps also received a Jane Addams Book Award for *Story of the Negro*.[12]

After Bontemps retired as head librarian at Fisk University, he stayed on as director of university relations and as acting librarian. In 1966, he decided to teach at the University of Illinois in Chicago.[13]

Three years later Bontemps became director of the Afro-American program at Yale University in New Haven, Connecticut. He was the curator of the James Weldon Johnson collection and worked extensively with the collection for his own in-depth study of the Harlem Renaissance.

In 1971, Bontemps returned to Fisk as a writer-in-residence and began working on his autobiography. While there, he edited *The Harlem Renaissance Remembered*, published in 1972.

Bontemps received many awards in his lifetime for his writing. He received the Alexander Pushkin Poetry Prize in 1926 and 1927, an *Opportunity* Short Story Prize in 1932, a Julius Rosenwald Fellowship from 1938–1939 and from 1942–1943, and the Dow Award from the Society of Midland Authors in 1967 for *Anyplace But Here*.[14]

Arna Bontemps died suddenly on June 4, 1973, of a heart attack. Up until his death he had been working on his autobiography and a biography of Langston Hughes. Bontemps was buried at the Greenwood Cemetery in Nashville, Tennessee.

9

Countee Cullen
(1903–1946)

Countee Cullen was a major literary figure during the Harlem Renaissance. Although he often used racial issues as a theme in his writing, he wanted to be judged on his merits as a poet, not as a black poet. His classical education in literature is reflected in the style and form of his lyric poetry, which set his work apart from other writers of the period.

Countee Cullen was born Countee Porter on May 30, 1903. Information about his early life is incomplete; his parents are not named in his records. It is known that his father disappeared shortly after Countee was born. Countee's grandmother raised him.[1]

When Countee was fifteen, his grandmother died. The Reverend Frederick Cullen and his wife,

81

Countee Cullen

Carolyn, then unofficially adopted Countee. Although the adoption was never formalized legally, Countee took the name of "Cullen" anyway. Reverend Cullen was an influential minister at what was then the largest church in Harlem, the Salem Methodist Episcopal Church.[2]

Countee began writing poetry as early as elementary school, and he won several poetry contests. This encouraged him to choose writing as a career. His first published poem, "I Have a Rendezvous with Life," appeared in 1921 in *The Magpie*, the DeWitt Clinton High School literary magazine.

DeWitt Clinton, Countee's high school, was one of the best public schools in New York City. Countee, one of the few African-American students at the school, was a very good student. He was elected to the honor society and graduated with distinction in French, Latin, English, math, and history.[3]

In 1924, when Cullen was only twenty-one, his poems had already achieved recognition. They were published in four magazines targeted toward mostly white audiences: *Harper's, Century, American Mercury*, and *Bookman*.[4]

Unlike poet Langston Hughes, Cullen felt that poetry should not necessarily reflect the race of the poet. Still his writing formed "one of the important points of influence the Harlem Renaissance has had on Afro-American/Black American protest literature of the 40s and 50s, and the Civil Rights/Revolution literary expressions of the late 50s, 60s, and early 70s."[5]

Cullen often used both a classical style, such as the strict meter of a sonnet, and symbolism in his work. The style and form of much of his poetry differed from that of other poets of the Harlem Renaissance. He preferred the classical form to black rhythms and ideas.

Historian David Levering Lewis said that the American mainstream reading public expected poets of the Harlem Renaissance to write about "jungles, gamy sexual passions, and the psychic woe of being black. Countee Cullen's lyrical poetry was capable of satisfying all of these stereotypes and projections, as in the beautifully evocative of Africa 'Heritage' . . . the deeply morbid 'Nothing Endures,' and 'Requiescam.'"[6]

Charles S. Johnson, editor of the National Urban League (NUL) publication, *Opportunity*, wrote an essay for a 1954 symposium at Howard University. He was celebrating the thirtieth anniversary of the first *Opportunity* awards dinner. In "The Negro Renaissance and Its Significance," Johnson said, ". . . Cullen gave a classic beauty to the emotions of the race. . . ."[7]

Another Harlem Renaissance writer, Wallace Thurman, said he pictured Cullen at work with his "eyes on a page of Keats, fingers on typewriter, [and]

Artist Aaron Douglas created this woodcut for the October 1926 issue
of *Opportunity.* Cullen became assistant editor of the magazine in 1926.

mind frantically conjuring up African scenes. And there would of course be a Bible nearby."[8]

Cullen achieved success early in his career. In 1924, Cullen was the first black poet to be published in *Palms: A Magazine of Poetry*, with his poem "Ballad of the Brown Girl." Even earlier, the Empire Federation Women's Clubs had named him New York's best young poet.[9]

In 1925, he graduated from New York University and was elected to Phi Beta Kappa (a national honor society). Cullen then went on to Harvard University where he received a master of arts degree in 1926.

Harper published Cullen's first book of poetry, *Color*, in 1925. Both black and white critics applauded it. One critic from the *Yale Review* said that Cullen should not be compared to just "other Negro poets of the past and present: he must stand or fail beside Shakespeare and Keats and Masefield, Whitman and Poe and Robinson."[10]

Cullen, himself, agreed and had even made a similar statement in an earlier interview with Margaret Sperry of the *Brooklyn Daily Eagle*. "If I am going to be a poet at all, I am going to be a *poet* and not a *Negro* poet," he said. This sentiment was evidently lost on the interviewer or her editor. The interview appeared in an article entitled "Countee P. Cullen, Negro Boy Poet, Tells His Story."[11]

Cullen was very popular with the Talented Tenth, the elite group of the Harlem Renaissance. To them, Cullen represented a gentility within the Harlem

Renaissance and the best artistic values of the movement. His work was published prominently.

Cullen won virtually all the prizes available to him at the time. While at New York University, Cullen had won the Witter Brynnen Undergraduate Poetry Prize. In May of 1925, in the second *Opportunity* literary contest, Cullen won second prize for his poem "To One Who Said Me Nay." In addition to the *Opportunity* prizes, he also won the Amy Spingarn Award of *The Crisis* and the John Reed Memorial Prize of Poetry.

White patron Carl Van Vechten published a book called *Nigger Heaven* in 1926. He intended the book to be a sympathetic portrayal of the roles of blacks as entertainment for the whites. The book caused a huge controversy. Some understood what Van Vechten had intended. Others disapproved of a white man revealing the inside of the Harlem Renaissance. Cullen was one of them. He did not speak to Van Vechten for fourteen years after *Nigger Heaven* was published.

In 1926, Cullen became assistant editor of *Opportunity*. While working there, he wrote a column, "The Dark Tower," which featured articles and book reviews. In it, he supported other black writers' need for literary freedom but placed limits on his own. "To let art portray things as they are, no matter what the consequences, no matter who is hurt is a blind bit of philosophy. . . . Every phrase of Negro life should not be the white man's concern."[12]

Cullen continued to receive awards and prizes for his work. In 1927, he was the recipient of the Harmon Foundation Literary Award and a Guggenheim Fellowship for study abroad. That year he also published *Copper Sun*, his major collection of poems.[13] Cullen's only novel, *One Way to Heaven*, was published five years later. It received only mild reviews.

On April 9, 1928, Cullen married Yolande Du Bois, the only daughter of W.E.B. Du Bois. It was an arranged marriage; Cullen was gay. They divorced in 1930. Du Bois blamed the breakup of the marriage on his daughter, and he and Cullen remained close.

It was an approval that Cullen needed from someone of Du Bois's importance. For one thing, Cullen was acutely aware of the color hierarchy even within the black community itself. Cullen was self-conscious about his very dark skin. Many of the other elite intellectuals of the Harlem Renaissance could "pass" for white.

In 1934, Cullen returned to DeWitt Clinton High School to teach French. One of his students was James Baldwin, who went on to become a great writer. Cullen also taught French and English at Public School 139, Frederick Douglass Junior High School, for many years.

In addition to his teaching, Cullen concentrated on lyric poetry and focused his writing on themes of love and nature.[14] He also wrote several children's books.

Cullen and fellow writer Arna Bontemps collaborated on a play called *St. Louis Woman*, based on Bontemps's novel *God Sends Sunday*. Unfortunately, a few months before the play started its successful run on Broadway in 1946, Cullen died.

At the time of his death, Cullen had also been working on a volume of his favorite poems, intending to call it *On These I Stand*.[15] He died on January 9, 1946, of uremic poisoning. Carl Van Vechten and Paul Robeson, the singer, were pallbearers at the funeral.

Cullen's poetry was the only poetry read. No spirituals were sung. W.E.B. Du Bois, at seventy-eight, delivered the eulogy. He said, "Cullen's career was not finished. It did not culminate. It laid [a] fine, beautiful foundation, but the shape of the building never emerged. . . . "[16]

A branch of the New York Public Library at 136th Street is named for Countee Cullen, one of the best known and respected poets of his time.

Josephine Baker

10

Josephine Baker
(1906–1975)

One of the greatest entertainers of the twentieth century was Josephine Baker, who took the world by storm. However, her relationship with the United States could also be described as stormy. Her own country was not quite ready for her style of entertainment, especially when it came from an African-American woman. Baker ended up living most of her life in France.

Josephine Baker was born June 3, 1906, in the slums of St. Louis, Missouri. Her parents were not married. Her mother, Freda Josephine MacDonald, was a washerwoman, and her father was the drummer for a local band.

Freda had trouble making enough money to care for Josephine and her three younger children. When she was only eight years old, Josephine began to work as a maid in the homes of white people to help out her family. By the age of fourteen, Josephine had left home to marry, then divorce, her first husband. (Four more husbands would follow.)[1]

After her first divorce, Baker began to perform with a black vaudeville troupe. The effects of the Harlem Renaissance had begun to spread to Europe. Europeans became fascinated with African and African-American culture. Blacks had become the twentieth century's "Noble Savages," as the American Indians had been called in the nineteenth century. Being black became fashionable.[2]

Baker's big break in show business came in 1921. She gained the starring role in *Shuffle Along*, an all-black musical revue. The show featured Eubie Blake's music and Noble Sissle's lyrics. *Shuffle Along*, the first African-American musical, was originally written by African Americans Aubry Lyles and Flournoy Miller. It was produced, cast, and choreographed entirely by African Americans.

At first, Baker had not been given the starring role because she was too small, too thin, too funny, and too dark-skinned.[3] She was originally given the comic part of the "end girl." This role was supposed to be a comic character that couldn't follow the dance moves of the other girls in the chorus. Baker stole the show with her performance.

Sissle and Blake billed Baker as the "highest paid chorus girl in the world" for their new show in

1924, *The Chocolate Dandies*. For her finale, Baker abandoned the end girl role and danced the "Wedding Finale" scene in a satin gown that was slit all the way up the leg. Her performance took command of center stage.[4]

In 1925, Baker was offered a role in *La Revue Nègre*, which opened in Paris, France, on October 2 at the Théâtre des Champs-Elysées. Carolyn Dudley Reagan, a patron, sponsored the show. She wanted to bring "real" Negro music and dance to Europe.[5]

Baker's finale, called "La Danse de Sauvage" (dance of the savage), was a sensation. The nineteen-year-old Baker performed the Charleston dance wearing nothing but a girdle of feathers.[6] Critics called her the "black Venus." European audiences went wild over her performance and she became a sensation.

Baker continued to perform on stages across Europe. In April 1926, Baker opened at the Folies-Bergère, the Parisian music hall known for its entertainment spectacles. She sang and danced in musical revues. Although most famous for her near nudity, Baker also introduced many mainstream American dances and techniques to European audiences.

Baker's dance act was not the only exotic thing about her, however. She was often seen strolling the streets of Paris with her pet leopard, Chiquita. She also owned birds, monkeys, snakes, dogs, a turkey, and a pig. Paris in the 1920s was experiencing a movement called "Le Jazz Hot," where an attitude of "anything goes" prevailed.

Baker had many famous admirers, including the artist Pablo Picasso. Fashion designer Christian Dior created outfits for her himself, and writer Ernest Hemingway called Baker the most beautiful woman he had ever seen.

American audiences—and the American public, in general—were more conservative in their tastes. They were not ready for Baker's free spirit, her in-your-face earthiness. However, she was well received when she stuck to the parts calling for her to play the clown or the savage.

By the 1930s, Baker's act had become more refined. However, American white audiences were not yet ready to accept Baker as a sophisticated and glamorous entertainer. She performed with the Ziegfeld Follies in 1936 and received very bad reviews. Frustrated, Baker returned to Paris in 1937.

Baker married a French sugar broker named Jean Lion, but divorced him almost immediately.[7] She decided that she liked living in France where she was very appreciated and she gave up her U.S. citizenship and became a French citizen.

During World War II, Baker became an ambulance driver and intelligence liaison for the French Resistance, the group of French citizens who fought the Germans after France surrendered to Germany. Baker was awarded the Medal of the Resistance and the French Legion of Honor for her efforts.[8]

Baker received a warm reception in Europe as the effects of the Harlem Renaissance began to spread outside of the United States.

After the war, Baker married orchestra leader Jo Bouillon. She returned to the United States and was given a more welcome reception this time. Fellow African Americans applauded her heroism in Europe and her support of the budding civil rights movement in the United States. To show her support Baker refused to play in segregated theaters or to stay in segregated hotels.[9] Because of this and her other work, the National Association for the Advancement of Colored People (NAACP) named her the Most Outstanding Woman of the Year for 1951.

In 1963, Baker participated in the civil rights March on Washington. She also gave a concert at Carnegie Hall in New York City to benefit the NAACP, the Student Nonviolent Coordinating Committee (SNCC), and the Congress of Racial Equality.[10]

In her personal life, Baker began actively to pursue the one role that had eluded her—being a mother. She was not able to have children of her own, so she decided to create a family through adoption. Between 1954 and 1965, she adopted children of many races and nationalities—two daughters and ten sons in all. She called her family the "Rainbow Tribe."[11]

Originally, Baker planned to retire to enjoy her family in her French château, Les Milandes. Unfortunately, she had run through her savings and couldn't support her large family. Their expenses forced her into debt, and she lost her château in 1969 to foreclosure. To help out, Princess Grace of Monaco—a former American actress known as Grace Kelly before her marriage to Prince Rainier— gave Baker a small villa in the principality of Monaco.[12]

Baker's last five years were a combination of public applause and personal misery. Back home in France, Baker had to resort to begging on the streets to feed her family. Without her stage makeup and glamorous designer outfits no one recognized her.

Baker was also beginning to fail physically. She had two heart attacks and a stroke. In spite of this, she still continued to perform. On stage she appeared to be the same Josephine Baker that the public had come to love.

A 1974 show called *Josephine* wowed audiences in Monaco. It moved to Paris in April of 1975, the fiftieth anniversary of Baker's Paris debut. On April 8, 1975, a huge gala celebrated her original arrival and her successful return. However, it was to be her final show.

On April 12, Baker had a cerebral hemorrhage and died while napping. She was sixty-eight years old. Over twenty thousand people attended her funeral in Paris. Josephine Baker was one of only a few performers ever given a state funeral.[13]

Although Josephine Baker did not seem to be an intimate part of the Harlem Renaissance, she was responsible to a great extent for the spread of the effects of the Harlem Renaissance beyond the United States' borders. Because of her work as a performer, audiences in many countries were treated to a glimpse of the New Negro.

Chapter Notes

Preface

1. Steven Watson, *The Harlem Renaissance* (New York: Pantheon Books, 1995), p. 9.

2. David Levering Lewis, ed., *The Portable Harlem Renaissance Reader* (New York: Viking Penguin, 1995), p. xiii.

3. Watson, p. 18.

4. Lewis, p. xxii.

5. Ibid., pp. xvii–xviii.

6. Langston Hughes, *The Big Sea* (New York: Hill and Wang, 1975), p. 228.

7. Ibid., p. 218.

8. Ibid., p. 247.

Chapter 1. James Weldon Johnson

1. Steven Watson, *The Harlem Renaissance* (New York: Pantheon Books, 1995), p. 21.

2. "Modern American Poetry," *James Weldon Johnson's Life and Career,* <http://english.uiuc.edu/maps/poets/g_l/johnson/life.htm> (February 5, 2002).

3. Watson, p. 21.

4. "The Academy of American Poets," *James Weldon Johnson,* <http://www.poets.org/Poets.cfm?prmID=73&CFID=2205298&CFTOKEN=77344655>, (February 8, 2002).

5. Watson, p. 21.

6. "Modern American Poets," <http://english.uiuc.edu/maps/poets/g_l/johnson/life.htm> (February 8, 2002).

7. Cary D. Wintz, *Black Culture and the Harlem Renaissance* (College Station, Tex.: Texas A&M University Press, 1996), p. 51.

8. "Modern American Poets," <http://english.uiuc. edu/maps/poets/g_l/johnson/life.htm> (February 8, 2002).

9. Watson, p. 21.

10. "James Weldon Johnson," *Poetry Exhibits,* <http://www.poets.org/poets/poets.cfm?prmID+73> (August 17, 2000).

11. David Levering Lewis, ed., *The Portable Harlem Renaissance Reader* (New York: Viking Penguin, 1995), p. 279.

12. Wintz, p. 3.

13. Ibid., p. 111.

14. Lewis, p. 207.

Chapter 2. Alain LeRoy Locke

1. "Alain Leroy Locke," Lisa Clayton Robinson, contributor, <http://www.africana.com/tt_164.htm> (September 10, 2000).

2. David Levering Lewis, ed., *The Portable Harlem Renaissance Reader* (New York: Viking Penguin, 1995), p. 206.

3. Cary D. Wintz, *Black Culture and the Harlem Renaissance* (College Station Tex.: Texas A&M University Press, 1996), p. 112.

4. Robinson.

5. Ibid.

6. Wintz, p. 112.

7. Robinson.

8. Wintz, p. 1.

9. Ibid., p. 30.

10. Ibid., p. 117.

11. Ibid., p. 118.

12. Lewis, p. 134.

13. Alain Locke, "Self-Criticism: The Third Dimension in Culture," *Phylon* 11, December 1950, p. 392. Cited in Wintz, p. 114.

14. Robinson.

15. Ibid.

16. Ibid.

Chapter 3. Zora Neale Hurston

1. Steven Watson, *The Harlem Renaissance* (New York: Pantheon Books, 1995), p. 70.

2. Zora Neale Hurston, *Dust Tracks on a Road* (New York: HarperCollins, 1995), p. 69.

3. Ibid., p. 135.

4. Ibid., p. 138.

5. Ibid.

6. Watson, pp. 66–67.

7. Hurston, p. 142.

8. Watson, p. 88.

9. Ibid., p. 149.

10. Ibid., p. 153.

11. Ibid., p. 162.

12. Hurston, p. 171.

13. Ibid., p. 305.

14. Watson, p. 170.

15. Hurston, p. 307.

16. Ibid.

17. Watson, p. 172.

Chapter 4. Bessie Smith

1. Henry Louis Gates, Jr., and Cornel West, *The African American Century* (New York: The Free Press, 2000), p. 109.

2. "Bessie Smith," <http://blueflamecafe.com/Bessie_Smith.html> (January 31, 2001).

3. Ibid.

4. "Bessie Smith Biography," <http://mathrisc1.lunet.edu/Bessie_Smith.html> (January 31, 2001).

5. Steven Watson, *The Harlem Renaissance* (New York: Pantheon Books, 1995), p. 120.

6. "Bessie Smith," <http://blueflamecafe.com/Bessie_Smith.html>

7. Gates, p. 111.

8. "Bessie Smith Biography," <http://mathrisc1.lunet.edu/Bessie_Smith.html>

9. Watson, p. 120.

10. "Bessie Smith," <http://blueflamecafe.com/Bessie_Smith.html>

11. Gates, p. 109.

12. Ibid., p. 111.

13. "Bessie Smith," <http://blueflamecafe.com/Bessie_Smith.html>

14. Watson, p. 120.

15. "Bessie Smith," <http://blueflamecafe.com/Bessie_Smith.html>

16. "Bessie Smith," (1895-1937), <http://redhotjazz.com/bessie.html> (January 31, 2001).

17. "Bessie Smith Biography," <http://mathrisc1.lunet.edu/Bessie_Smith.html>

18. "Bessie Smith," (1895-1937), <http://redhotjazz.com/bessie.html> (January 31, 2001).

19. Gates, p. 109.

20. "Bessie Smith," <http://www.greatwomen.org/profile.php?id=145> (February 13, 2002).

Chapter 5. Aaron Douglas

1. David Levering Lewis, ed., *The Portable Harlem Renaissance Reader* (New York: Viking Penguin, 1995), p. 119.

2. Steven Watson, *The Harlem Renaissance* (New York: Pantheon Books, 1995), p. 89.

3. Watson, p. 90.

4. Henry Louis Gates, Jr., and Cornel West, *The African American Century* (New York: The Free Press, 2000), p. 26.

5. Lewis, p. 747.

6. Public Broadcasting Service video, *Against the Odds: The Artists of the Harlem Renaissance*, PBS Home Video, 1994.

7. Ibid.

8. Lewis, pp. 121-122.

9. Cary D. Wintz, *Black Culture and the Harlem Renaissance* (College Station, Tex.: Texas A&M University Press, 1996), p. 83.

10. "Artnoir's African/American Art, History 101," Aaron Douglas (1899-1979), <http://www.artnoircom/index.douglas.aaron.html> (February 8, 2002).

11. "Aaron Douglas (1899-1979)," <http://www.si.umich.edu/CHICO/Harlem/text/adouglas.html> (August 22, 2000).

12. Lewis, p. 740.

Chapter 6. Duke Ellington

1. "The Duke Ellington Appreciation Society," <http://duke.fuse.net/misc/family.html> (January 26, 2001).

2. Henry Louis Gates, Jr., and Cornel West, *The African American Century* (New York: The Free Press, 2000), p. 159.

3. "Edward Kennedy 'Duke' Ellington" (1899–1974), <http://www.si.umich.edu/CHICO/Harlem/text/ellington.html> (December 18, 2000).

4. Ibid.

5. Gates, p. 161.

6. Steven Watson, *The Harlem Renaissance: Hub of African-American Culture, 1920–1930* (New York: Pantheon Books, 1995), p. 126.

7. Ibid., p. 112.

8. Ibid., p. 109.

9. Gates, p. 161.

10. "Edward Kennedy 'Duke' Ellington" (1899–1974), <http://www.si.umich.edu/CHICO/Harlem/text/ellington.html> (December 18, 2000).

11. Gates, p. 161.

12. "The Duke Ellington Appreciation Society," <http://duke.fuse.net/misc/family.html> (January 26, 2001).

13. Gates, p. 163.

14. Ibid.

15. Ibid.

16. "Edward K. 'Duke' Ellington," <http://www.schirmer.com/composers/ellington_bio.html> (January 26, 2001).

17. "The Duke Ellington Appreciation Society," <http://duke.fuse.misc/hajdu.html> (January 26, 2001).

18. "Edward K. 'Duke' Ellington," <http://www.schirmer.com/composers/ellington_bio.html> (January 26, 2001).

Chapter 7. Langston Hughes

1. Langston Hughes, *The Big Sea* (New York: Hill and Wang, 1975), p. 14.

2. Ibid., p. 40.

3. Ibid., p. 39.

4. Ibid., p. 56.
5. Ibid., p. 11.
6. Ibid., p. 205.
7. Ibid., p. 266.
8. Ibid., pp. 226–227.

Chapter 8. Arna Bontemps

1. "Arna Wendell Bontemps" (1902–1973), <http://falcon.jmu.edu/~ramseyil/bontemps.htm> (September 4, 2000).

2. "Arna Bontemps" (1902–1973), <http://www.bedfordstmartins.com/litlinks/fiction/.htm> (February 12, 2002).

3. "Arna Wendell Bontemps" (1902–1973), <http://falcon.jmu.edu/~ramseyil/bontemps.htm> (September 4, 2000).

4. David Levering Lewis, ed., *The Portable Harlem Renaissance Reader* (New York: Viking Penguin, 1995), p. xxviii.

5. Langston Hughes, *The Big Sea* (New York: Hill and Wang, 1975), p. 248.

6. Cary D. Wintz, *Black Culture and the Harlem Renaissance* (College Station, Tex.: Texas A&M University Press, 1996), p. 219.

7. "Arna Wendell Bontemps" (1902–1973), <http://www.falcon.jmu.edu/~ramseyil/bontemps.htm> (September 4, 2000).

8. Linda T. Wynn, <http://picard.tnstate.edu/~library/digital/Bontemp.htm> (January 29, 2001).

9. Lewis, p. 667.

10. Wynn.

11. Ibid.

12. "Arna Wendell Bontemps" (1902–1973), <http:// falcon.jmu.edu/~ramseyil/bontemps.htm> (September 4, 2000).

13. Wynn.

14. "The Life and Times of Arna Wendell Bontemps," <http://www.arnabontempsmuseum.com> (February 12, 2002).

Chapter 9. Countee Cullen

1. Steven Watson, *The Harlem Renaissance* (New York: Pantheon Books, 1995), p. 48.

2. "Countee Cullen," <http://www.si.umich.edu/ CHICO/Harlem/wam/search.html> (February 12, 2002).

3. Ibid.

4. Watson, p. 78.

5. Homer L. Meade, Ph.D., Ed.D., in personal communication with the author (December 20, 2000).

6. David Levering Lewis, ed., *The Portable Harlem Renaissance Reader* (New York: Viking Penguin, 1995), p. 242.

7. Ibid., p. 211.

8. Wallace Thurman, *Infants of the Spring* (New York: Macaulay, 1932), p. 236.

9. Watson, p. 48.

10. Clement Wood, "The Negro Sings," *Yale Review*, July 15, 1926, p. 824.

11. Margaret Sperry, "Countee P. Cullen, Negro Boy Poet, Tells His Story," *Brooklyn Daily Eagle*, February 10, 1924, p. 78.

12. Cary D. Wintz, *Black Culture and the Harlem Renaissance* (College Station, Tex.: Texas A&M University Press, 1996), p. 152.

13. "Countee Cullen," <http://www.si.umich.edu/ CHICO/Harlem/wam/search.html> (February 12, 2002).

14. Ibid.

15. Watson, p.168.

16. W.E.B. Du Bois, "The Winds of Time," *Chicago Defender,* January 1946, p. 169.

Chapter 10. Josephine Baker

1. Lisa Clayton Robinson, contributor <http://www. africana. com/tt_036.htm> (September 10, 2000).

2. Steven Watson, *The Harlem Renaissance* (New York: Pantheon Books, 1995), p. 105.

3. Ibid., p. 110.

4. Henry Louis Gates, Jr., and Cornel West, *The African American Century* (New York: The Free Press, 2000), p. 85.

5. Ibid.

6. Robinson.

7. Gates, p. 89.

8. Robinson.

9. Ibid.

10. Ibid.

11. Ibid.

12. Ibid.

13. Gates, p. 89.

Further Reading

Hill, Christine M. *Langston Hughes: Poet of the Harlem Renaissance.* Springfield, N.J.: Enslow Publishers, Inc., 1997.

Hughes, Langston. *The First Book of Jazz.* Hopewell, N.J.: The Ecco Press, 1982.

Marvis, B., and Veronica Chambers. *The Harlem Renaissance.* New York: Chelsea House Publishers, 1997.

McKissack, Patricia, and Fredrick McKissack. *James Weldon Johnson: "Lift Every Voice and Sing."* Chicago: Children's Press, 1991.

Pinkney, Andrea Davis. *Duke Ellington: The Piano Prince and His Orchestra.* New York: Hyperion, 1998.

Rennert, Richard. *Shapers of America: Profiles of Great Black Americans.* New York: Chelsea House Publishers, 1994.

Internet Addresses

The Harlem Renaissance
<http://www.usc.edu/isd/archives/ethnicstudies/
   harlem.html>

**The Harlem Renaissance: Life, Movement,
Creativity, Revolution**
<http://www.nku.edu/~diesmanj/harlem.html>

**Harlem 1900–1940: An African-American
Community**
<http://www.si.umich.edu/CHICO/Harlem/>

Index